NOODLES, NITWITS, AND NUMSKULLS

By the Same Author

THE THING AT THE FOOT OF THE BED

THE RAINBOW BOOK OF
AMERICAN FOLK TALES AND LEGENDS

MARIA LEACH

Noodles, Nitwits,
and Numskulls

DRAWINGS BY *Kurt Werth*

COLLINS

For Kennie
who makes up his own jokes

Published by William Collins Publishers Incorporated.
2080 West 117th Street, Cleveland, Ohio 44111

Library of Congress Catalog Card Number: 61-14112
ISBN 0-529-03662-2
13P1278

Copyright © 1961 by Maria Leach

Contents

TRICKS

SURPRISES AND ANSWERS

Yesterday—and Forever

THE JOKES in this book are the eternal jokes of the human mind, centuries old but forever turning up as just having happened. Some relative or friend of yours has a friend who knows the man it happened to. And the teller usually believes what he tells: it *did* happen, just the other day, to the friend of a friend; or his cousin's neighbor's child did say that clever thing.

This is the way of the folk with a joke—so much so that some scholars say there is no such thing as an unknown joke. Old jokes never die. They just keep popping up with new trimmings.

Today we have jokes about the absent-minded professor and discover that most of them were told hundreds of years ago about some ancient Greek or Chinese or Persian learned man. The American Little Moron earnestly repeats the same blunders of the ancient Indian or Turkish or Sicilian boobies. The story of the hansom-cab driver on Fifty-ninth Street south of Central Park in New York City, whose horse died just when he got it trained to go without food, is descended from countless cabbies in the world who have had the same experience for centuries—ever since the fifth century B.C., in fact.

The little town of Gotham in England was not the only little town in the world famous for the behavior of its inhabitants. There were the stupid men of Abdera in Thrace (fifth century B.C.); the silly Schildbergers (Germany); the people of Belmont (Switzerland); the men of ancient Emesa (or Homs) in Syria, whose antics were immortalized in Arabic and Persian stories; and the people of Chelm (Poland), whose absurdities set the type for European Yiddish jokes. There were stupid Brahman tales in India, Silly Matt tales in Norway, and other silly son stories all over Europe.

Most of the stories in this book seem to take place in little far-off villages, on lonely roads remote from railway or highway, and in the palaces of little local kings. If they seem not to touch closely on today's daily life, it is because they are timeless; they belong to no place—but to the human mind. The story elements, the motifs, the little plots, are centuries old; and many of them are almost world-wide. Thus the settings (elemental, almost abstract) do not color or intrude upon the humor.

It is interesting to note that the riddles, too, are for the most part basic and elemental. *How far is it to the bottom of the sea? How far around the earth? How far between heaven and earth?* These are the same questions that mankind is still trying to answer—even to the extent of hurling men into space to find out.

The same things can be said about the tricks and sells and traps and tests and hoaxes in the world. Holding down the hat, holding up the cliff, holding the glass of water to the ceiling; these tricks have been played on the unwary for centuries on three continents and many islands. It would be fun to know how many people in how many little towns have spent how much money to see the wonderful horse with his head where his tail ought to be, from ancient Persian times, through the Middle Ages in Europe, and into modern America.

As for the deadpan story with the surprise ending, perhaps the one from the Siberian Eskimos is the most amazing; it is certainly the most subtle. There is the serious little boy gathering seaweed, confronted with the serious problem of getting through the little door, and the serious grandmother presenting him with the eye of a needle through which to enter and—*through which he enters.*

The notes in the back of the book make some attempt to say briefly where the stories and riddles come from and to indicate their spread. The motif numbers are included for anyone who may be interested in following through with further reading.

Guess how many eggs I have and
I'll give you all seven

NOODLES

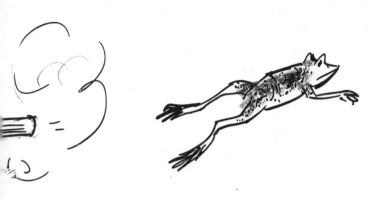

The Man with the Chair
on His Head

ONCE there was a couple of fellows who went deer hunting together.

One was a countryman and knew all about it; the other was from the city and had never even seen a deer. But that was all right: the city visitor said he would do just as he was told.

So the country fellow gave the city fellow a gun and took him off into the woods. He told him to stand in a certain place while he went off with the dogs to start the deer.

"Shoot the first thing you see making big jumps," he said. "Then blow your horn and I'll come."

Well, the fellow stood there a while and saw nothing. Then a frog came leaping out of the bushes to get away from a snake. That was a big jump all right—so the city fellow shot him. Then he blew the horn to notify his friend.

While he was waiting, a real deer came running by—a big buck with a fine pair of antlers.

"Did you get him? Did you get him?" said the country fellow when he came along.

"Yes, I got him!" The city man pointed to the frog.

"That's not a deer!" said the other. "Didn't a deer come running this way?"

"No. Nobody came by here except a man with a chair on his head."

Dreams

1. *Bear Hunt*

DID YOU HEAR about the man who dreamed he went hunting? He dreamed he was hunting a bear and when he caught up with it, the bear turned and chased him. He was terrified. In fact this dream frightened him so much that the next night he took the dog to bed with him.

This must be the same man who took a mirror to bed with him one night so he could see whether or not he slept with his mouth open.

2. *Three Dreams*

Once three young men went hunting in the woods and took along another to be cook. They hunted all day long without stopping to eat, and when evening came they had caught nothing but one partridge.

One little bird was not enough for four hungry men, so they hit upon a plan. They would save the partridge for breakfast, and whoever dreamed the best dream in the night should have it. Then they went to sleep.

Morning came.

"What did you dream?" each asked the other.

"Oh, I dreamed that I married the most beautiful princess in the world," said one.

That was a wonderful dream, they all agreed.

"I dreamed that I saw my dear old mother," said the second.

"Ah, better yet!" they said.

"I," said the third, "I dreamed that I was in heaven and saw God himself."

This dream was even better. They all had to admit that.

"As for me," said the cook, "I dreamed that I ate the partridge. And the dream must be true, because I can't find it!"

Do It Yourself

ONE NIGHT a man on his way home from a party took a short cut across a field instead of going round by the road.

He was walking along confidently when suddenly he fell into a newly dug hole. He tried to climb up one side of it, but the loose earth slid down around his feet. He kept trying, but the more he tried, the deeper in he got.

He tried the other side, but the earth was loose there too, and he soon found himself buried to the knees.

He tried again and again, and the loose soil kept sliding down, and he just could *not* get out. So he gave up and went home to get a shovel to dig himself out.

Catching the Thief

TWO SILLY FELLOWS were sleeping together one night when a thief crept in and pulled the quilt off them and ran away with it.

"Run after him!" said one. "Run get the quilt!"

"Don't be foolish!" said the other. "Wait till he comes back for the pillow, and we'll both jump on him!"

Telling the Horses Apart

ONCE there were two fools who used to go horse-back riding together, but they never could tell their horses apart.

So one of them docked his horse's tail. That was fine: now one had a long tail and one had a short tail. The fools could tell them apart.

Then one day the long-tailed horse got his tail caught in a gate, and after that the two tails were the same length.

So one fool put a notch in his horse's ear. Now one horse had a notched ear and the other didn't, and it was easy to tell the horses apart.

Then one day the other horse notched his ear on a wire fence, and after that their ears were alike.

Finally the two fools thought of measuring the horses! And they discovered that the white horse was two inches taller than the black horse. After that they had no trouble.

Shoes Don't Match

ONE DAY a very high Chinese judge was walking along and he noticed that he was limping. He was not a lame man. Why did he limp? His leg didn't even hurt. So he looked down at his feet.

Right away he saw what was the matter. His shoes didn't match! One was a fine boot with a rather high heel. The other was less dressy—and flat.

So he told the clerk who attended him to go home and hurry back with the right shoe.

The clerk rushed off but in a few minutes came back empty-handed. "It is no use to change your shoes," he said sadly. "The pair at home are just like these."

What is it has a soul that can't be saved?

A SHOE (SOLE)

Two boats with only one man aboard. What is it?

A PAIR OF SHOES ON ONE MAN

Trip to Town

TWO YOUNG FELLOWS were standing by the side of the road, waiting for the bus. They had errands in town.

They waited and they waited. The bus was late—and they waited.

Finally one young fellow said, "If that bus doesn't come soon, I'm going to go to town in the wheelbarrow."

"You can't do that," said the other. "How will you make it go?"

"Run along behind it."

This Nova Scotia anecdote is close kin to the European one about the man who straddled the stick hobbyhorse and trotted all the way into town. He said he was just as tired as if he had walked.

The Wrong Man

THREE MEN went traveling a long road on foot together. One was a very learned man, one was bald, and one was a barber. Each carried a few valuables with him, so they agreed to take turns keeping watch in the night.

It was the barber's turn first. He got tired sitting there awake by himself, so to amuse himself he shaved all the hair off the learned man's head.

It was the scholar's turn to keep watch next, so when the time came, the barber woke him. The scholar put up his hands to smooth his hair—and felt a bare head!

"Fool of a barber!" he exclaimed. "He has wakened the bald man instead of me!"

25

Silly John

SILLY JOHN is the boy who took the lamp outdoors when his mother told him to "put out the light." And one day as she left the house to go to market, she told John to dress the chicken for dinner. When she got back, there was the hen all dressed up in one of the baby's dresses, sitting in the baby's high chair with a ribbon round its neck.

One day the mother sent John to the store to buy some needles. "Get size number seven," she said.

So John went to the store and got the needles all right. On his way home he passed a pond, and the frogs were yelling, *Eight-eight, eight-eight.*

"You're wrong!" cried Silly John. "They're number seven!"

Eight-eight, eight-eight! yelled the frogs and kept it up.

"It's seven! It's seven!" cried John. "Here! See for yourselves!" And he threw the package of needles into the pond.

When John got home, his mother said, "Where are the needles?"

"Oh, Mother! The frogs kept saying they were number eight! So I threw them in the pond to prove they were size seven. And they wouldn't give them back."

The Louisiana Cajuns and Creoles tell another tale

about Silly John (whom they call Jean Sot). One day the king said, "They tell me, Jean, that Compair Lapin is your father." (*Compair* means "comrade.")

"That is true," said Jean. "He is my father."

"But I thought Compair Bouki was your father."

"Yes. He is my father also."

Just then an old woman passed by and overheard the conversation.

"No," she said. "Renard is your father."

"Oh, yes," said Jean. "He, too. Every day one of them says, 'Good day, my child.' They are all my fathers."

27

Chestnuts

D<small>ID YOU HEAR</small> about the little moron who saw the headline in the paper *Americans Fight with Axis* and then went around collecting money to buy guns and ammunition for the soldiers?

The little moron was born in America in the 1930's and grew up during World War II, but he was already centuries old at birth. Old jokes never die. People not only love their old jokes, but people everywhere love the same ones! Little Moron is just another name for the beloved world-wide fool, booby, noodle, or numskull.

There were two little morons who went fishing and caught so many fish that they wished they could find the same place the next day. "We'll find it," said one little moron. "I put a mark on the boat right over the place we were fishing."

"But how do you know we'll get this same boat tomorrow?"

This story seems to have been told all over the world wherever any two people ever went fishing together. It is as old as the early Buddhistic writings in India and China. It was current all over Europe in the Middle Ages and is now told almost everywhere in North America as having been said by "an old man my grandfather knew."

One little moron was telling another his terrible

dream. He dreamed that he stepped on a nail which pierced his foot. "Well, why do you sleep barefoot?" said the other.

This one is at least 1,400 years old. It is one of the jests of the Greek sage Hierocles of the fifth century A.D., whose jests were already chestnuts, from India and perhaps Egypt, when he recorded them. The chestnut about the man whose horse died just as he got it trained to live without food is also one of the jests of Hierocles. It was common throughout Europe long before it spread to America as one of hundreds of pointed little anecdotes all beginning with the words "Did you hear about the man who . . . ?"*

Lots of the Silly John (Jean Sot) tales are also very ancient. In one of these, Silly John's mother left him at home to guard the door, and he just took it off the hinges and carried it with him when he went out. This story was told about Giufa, the Sicilian booby, at least three hundred years ago.

Then there are the men of Gotham: the wise men, the mad men of Gotham. Stories of their doings were told hundreds of years ago, too, as jokes about ancient Greek sages or the Turkish fool Khoja Nasreddin of the fourteenth century. And some are centuries older than that—tales about noodles and their blunders— stemming from India. How their pranks came to be attached to the inhabitants of the little English town of Gotham is told in the next story.

* From *The Rainbow Book of American Folk Tales and Legends* by Maria Leach, The World Publishing Company, 1958. By permission of the publishers.

The Wise Men of Gotham

THE WISE MEN of Gotham were a bunch of fools. Noodles and nitwits and numskulls some people call them. And jokes about them have been told and retold for about seven hundred years—ever since King John and his men tried to ride through the town of Gotham in Nottinghamshire, England, one day in the thirteenth century.

And some people say that the men of Gotham were wise and wily and not fools at all. They knew the old law whereby any piece of ground over which the king traveled must henceforth be a public road.

They did not *want* a public road through Gotham, so they went forth and piled logs across the way of the royal party and would not let them enter the village.

King John was so enraged at this impudence that he sent deputies into Gotham to find out why the people had been so inhospitable to their king.

And what did the deputies see? They saw three men trying to drown an eel in the town pond. They saw a group of workmen carrying sunlight in wheelbarrows into a church without windows. They saw another group beside a garden wall lamenting noisily. When asked why they lamented, they explained that they had set up this fine wall around a garden to pen in a cuckoo so that Gotham might have summer all the year round. (Everybody knows, of course, that the song of the cuckoo brings sum-

31

mer.) They had promised the bird a life of comfort
and plenty. But the minute they let it loose inside
the wall, it flew away.

"We were fools," they said, "not to have made the
wall higher."

Another tale is that one of the king's men came
upon twelve men on a river bank searching for one
of their group who had drowned. They had all been
swimming; and when they came out on the river
bank, one of them said, "I pray God that none of us
is drowned."

"Well, let's count," said another. "There should
be twelve of us."

So he made the first count, and he counted eleven.

"Eleven!" he said. "*You* count," he said to the next
man.

That man counted and he counted eleven.

"Eleven!" he said. "Oh! One of us is surely

drowned! *You* count," he said to the man next to him.

So that man counted, and he too counted eleven. They all counted and each one came out with eleven.

"Oh! One of us is drowned!" they said. And they ran up and down the river bank, looking for some sign of their lost comrade.

A man on horseback came along just then and asked what was the matter.

"We came here twelve, to go swimming," they said. "And now we are eleven. One of us is drowned."

"Well, count again," said the horseman. So they counted again, and again they counted out eleven.

"What will you pay if I find the twelfth man?"

"Every cent we've got," said the men of Gotham.

"You first!" the stranger said to one and gave him a sharp cut with his whip. "This makes one!" he said.

And thus he went through the twelve—for each man, when he counted, had forgotten to count himself.

When the horseman came to the last man, he struck him sharply with the whip, and the man cried out.

"Here is the twelfth man," he said.

And the men of Gotham thanked the stranger and blessed him from their hearts for finding their lost companion.

So the deputies went back to King John and said it was no use trying to reason with the men of Gotham: they were a bunch of fools.

Were they?

Drowning the Eel

ONE DAY the men of Gotham got together to decide what to do with all the extra salt fish they had. And they agreed it would be a good thing to cast them all into the town pond where they might breed and multiply for the coming year.

"I have a lot of white herring," said one.

"I have red herring," said the next.

"Mine are sprats," said a third.

"Well, let us go and cast them into the pond, and we'll have abundance next year."

So they did. Each man threw all his leftover salt fish into the pond.

A year went by and they went to the pond to get their fish. They fished and caught nothing but one great big eel.

"This wicked eel has eaten all our fish!" they said.

"What shall we do with him?" said one.

"Wring his neck!"

"Chop him up in little pieces!"

"No," said a third man. "Let's drown him."

That seemed the best thing to do, so they threw the eel into the pond to drown.

A Fine Cheese

ONE NIGHT one of the men of Gotham came home late and saw what he took for a huge cheese in the pond near his house. He ran from door to door and woke up all his neighbors. "Come help get the cheese out of the pond!" he cried.

They came running with rakes, and they raked and raked but could not get it.

All of a sudden the moon went under a cloud, and the cheese disappeared. It sank, they said. They were bitterly disappointed, for it looked like a fine cheese.

This story reminds us of the Lithuanian riddle:

A pancake is lying in the well.

THE MOON

Lightening the Load

ANOTHER MAN of Gotham, kindhearted fellow, was riding home one day from a mill where he had bought a big sack of meal. He rode with the sack flung before him across the ass's back.

After a while in the heat of the day, he thought the poor ass must be exhausted with the weight of the load. So he lifted up the sack and laid it across his own shoulders.

"That will lighten the load," he said.

This story is told also about an Irishman with a keg of rum in a boat. The boat was full of people and their luggage, all being ferried across a river. The ferryman was worried and remarked that the small boat was overloaded. So the Irishman lifted his keg up onto his shoulder to lighten the load.

I Was Wondering

ONCE there was a man making a journey on horse-back with his servant. At night he warned the boy to keep careful watch over the horse.

Before going to sleep himself, he wanted to make sure the boy was awake.

"Caspar, are you asleep?"

"No, I was wondering who put so many stars in the sky."

After a while the man turned in his sleep and asked again, "Caspar, are you asleep?"

"No, I was wondering who dug the sea. It fills a big hole. Where did he put all the earth?"

Later the man asked again, "Caspar, are you asleep?"

"No, I was wondering who would carry the saddle now that the horse is gone."

Rescuing the Moon

ONCE there was a man who saw the moon reflected in the water in a pond near-by his house. He ran and got a rope and tried to pull the moon out, but he could not seem to get the rope around it.

Then he ran and got a net. That would do it, he thought. He cast the net again and again but never succeeded in dragging the moon out of the pond. And finally, he fell in himself.

He had a hard time getting out, for the bank was steep and wet and slippery. But in the midst of his struggle to get out, the man looked up, and there was the moon in the sky.

"Anyway, the moon is saved," he said.

RIDDLES

What is it that nobody wants but wouldn't give up if he had it?

A BALD HEAD

A Riddle Is a Wonderful Thing

SOLVING a riddle brings good luck to the solver. Guessing the answer to a hard riddle, unaided, always results in some good thing. Even today some people still tell riddles at the dinner table on New Year's Day to bring prosperity and good luck to the guessers for the coming year.

All through the folktales of the world, only good befalls the guesser of a riddle. Success and the heart's desire come quickly on the heels of a right answer.

The youth who can outriddle the princess is always given her hand in marriage. There are also many tales of the clever peasant girl being asked riddles by the king. Or a king invents riddles and puzzles to test the cleverness of a person or a populace and marries the young girl who gives the right answers or solves the puzzle.

In one of these the king gives a feast and invites everybody in the kingdom. But—the guests must come neither naked nor clad. The cleverest one, of course, is the young girl who comes wrapped up in a fish net. And sometimes a king asks riddles of his sons to find out which one will make the wisest successor to the throne.

Sometimes it is even a matter of life and death. Death was the penalty for failing to answer the riddle of the Sphinx, for instance.

The criminal about to be hanged is pardoned if he can make up a riddle that the king or the judge or the executioner cannot answer. These are called *neck riddles* because they save necks. And there are tales of escape from the Devil himself by answering the Devil's riddles.

Riddling is a magic charm, too, to bring rain in times of terrible drought.

What is a golden plow worth?

A RAIN IN MAY

The arrows of God cannot be counted.

RAIN

44

The Riddle of the Sphinx

NOBODY can say "riddle" without somebody saying "Sphinx," because the riddle of the Sphinx is one of the oldest and most famous riddles in the world.

What is it that goes on four legs in the morning, on two legs at midday, and on three legs in the evening?

That is the riddle of the Sphinx.

The Sphinx was an ancient Greek mythological monster with the head and face of a beautiful maiden and the body of a winged lion. She sat on a high rock outside the city of Thebes in Greece and stopped passers-by.

She stopped all who came along and asked her riddle. (Some of the old poets say she sang her riddle.) If they could not answer it, she devoured them and threw the bones off the rock into the valley below.

If anyone ever answered the riddle, the spell would be broken: The Sphinx would perish and the city would be saved. But nobody could answer the riddle. The city of Thebes was in a desperate plight.

Finally the people said that whoever could answer the riddle of the Sphinx was to be king of Thebes and marry the queen. But those who were tempted to go out and try their luck never came back.

Then one day along came a young hero named Oedipus. He was foster son to the king of Corinth

45

and had left that court to go traveling through the world.

When he came to Thebes, the Sphinx stopped him.

"What is it," she said, "that goes on four legs in the morning, on two legs at midday, and on three legs in the evening?"

"Oh, *that*," said Oedipus, "that is man—who crawls on all fours as a baby, walks on two legs as a man, and uses two legs and a stick in old age."

It was the right answer.

The Sphinx gave a shriek and hurled herself from her high place and was dashed to pieces on the rocks below.

Thus Oedipus answered the riddle, saved Thebes from the Sphinx, and was proclaimed king. What happened to Oedipus after that is another story.

Seven Sons

ONCE there was an old woman who had seven sons. They somehow all got into trouble at once and were going to be hanged.

The old woman went to the king to plead for their lives. But the king said no, they would be hanged for their crimes unless she could spin a riddle he could not guess.

So the poor old woman went into the woods and sat down to think. She did not know how to make up a riddle.

Then she saw a woodpecker go into a hole in a tree. In a minute he came out again.

And then it came to her:

> In it went
> Out it come
> And saved the lives
> Of seven sons

The next day was the terrible day when the old woman's seven young sons were to be put to death. So she went to the king and said:

> In it went
> Out it come
> And saved the lives
> Of seven sons

47

The king thought and thought and could not think what it was. It never entered his head to say "woodpecker."

So it was a riddle the king could not guess, and the seven sons were saved.

The Full Moon

THE KING ordered the cook to make a big round tart, as big as a dinner plate, and thirty small cakes. And he ordered a capon to be roasted. When they were done, he sent them with his servant to a clever, clever girl.

The next day he sent for the girl and asked her three questions.

"Is it full moon?" he said.

"No. It is half moon," said the girl.

"Is it the thirtieth of the month?"

"No. It is the fifteenth of the month."

"Did the cock crow in the evening?"

"No. The cock has been through the mill."

From these answers the king knew that the servant had eaten half the round tart, half the cakes, and all the capon. And then the girl made a fourth answer, and the fourth answer was a riddle itself: "Spare the pheasant for the sake of the partridge," she said.

The king was pretty clever himself. From this he knew she meant that he was not to punish the poor fellow too severely—for the sake of a kindhearted girl.

Outriddling the Princess

ONCE upon a time in some far country in some far time there was a princess called Smarty. Nobody liked her much.

She would not marry anyone who asked her, because she thought they were all too stupid. So the king and queen sent for the smartest riddler in the country. This was a very famous old man who knew a hard riddle for every day in the year.

"If he asks her three riddles she cannot answer, he shall have her for his wife," said the king.

"But he's a hundred years old!" cried the princess.

"No matter," said the king.

So the Riddler came, and all the people gathered in the throne room to hear the riddling.

The Riddler asked the princess riddles all morning long, and she guessed every one of them. He began with the easy ones and worked up to the hard ones. But Smarty knew all the answers.

So the king and queen said it was no use, the Riddler could go home. But the Riddler had saved his three hardest riddles for last.

"How far is it across the earth?" he said.

"A day's journey," said the princess.

"How's that?"

"The sun does it in a day," said the princess.

"What's this I see coming?" he cried, running to the window. "It has six legs, four ears, and two faces."

That was a new one. All the listeners thought the princess would have to give up. But she heard a horse galloping in the distance, and she thought fast.

"It's a horse and rider coming, with four legs on the horse and two on the man—makes six," said the princess, counting on her fingers, "and two ears on each—makes four—and each with his own face—makes two," she said.

"Right," said the Riddler sadly. "Here is one more. Today I saw one head with seven tongues in it."

"I saw that old horse skull, too!" said the princess. "It's in the field with a bird's nest in it and seven young ones in the nest and a tongue in each bird."

So the Riddler went home.

By this time the horse and rider had arrived at the palace gate. It was a young boy who had come to hear the riddling, but he was too late. The riddles were over. The Riddler was gone and the princess was sitting all alone in the big room. He thought she was very beautiful.

"Hello," said the boy.

"Go away, Stupid," said the princess.

"I'm as smart as you are," said the boy.

The princess hoped he was right, for it was a lonely life she led.

"I've come to marry you," said the boy.

"Then answer three riddles," said the princess.

"All right," said the boy.

"What bird sits in the top of that tree in the morning"—she pointed to the cypress east of the gate—"and in the top of that tree in the evening"—she pointed to the cypress west of the gate.

"That bird is the sun," said the boy.

The princess was surprised. No one could have told him the answer. It was a new riddle she had just made up herself.

"How far is it to the bottom of the sea?" she said.

"A stone's throw," said the boy.

"That's two he's answered," the king whispered to the queen. They were behind the door—listening.

"Then how far is it from this world to the next?" said the princess.

"One step," said the boy.

The princess's eyes popped wide. She had thought there could be no answer at all to that one.

"What?"

"Sure," said the boy. "Hasn't my grandfather had one foot in the grave for a year?"

"Hooray!" cried the king. The boy had correctly answered three riddles. So they announced the wedding for the next day.

The boy was very proud of his lovely, clever bride.

"What red lips you have," he said as they walked on the lawn.

"That's fire inside," said the princess—and stuck out her little red tongue.

"Then cook this egg," said the boy. And into her mouth he popped a blue robin's egg that he had picked up under a tree. That silenced her.

So the princess thought in her heart they were as smart as each other, and the wedding took place next day.

The Blind Men and the Elephant

FOUR BLIND MEN found an elephant and did not know what it was.

"It is like a log," said one, who had flung his arms around the elephant's leg.

"No! It is like a rope," said another, who had caught hold of its tail.

"It is more like a fan," said the third. He was feeling the shape of the elephant's ear.

"It is something with no beginning and no end," said the fourth, who was walking round and round the animal, feeling its sides.

"What is it?" they said.

This story is told in India of three blind men.

"It is like a water pipe," said one, feeling the elephant's trunk.

"It is like a fan," said another, who had hold of its ear.

"It is like a throne," said the third, who was feeling the high, broad side of the creature.

"What is it?"

Would anyone answer "Elephant"?

The House Without Eyes or Ears

LONG AGO a young king went forth early one day to call upon a certain young girl. When he arrived she was not ready for him. She had on some old thing; she was not dressed up in her fine bright clothes.

She was very much embarrassed, and she said to him, "The house has neither eyes nor ears."

From this riddle answer the young king knew there was no child in the house to look out the window and no dog keeping watch in the yard. So how could she know he was coming?

He was pleased with the riddle. And not only did he excuse her unreadiness, but he thought she was a pretty smart girl to think up a riddle like that.

With and Without

ONCE there was a young king who decided to give a great feast. He invited everybody in the kingdom. Everybody. But—each person had to come *with and without a present!*

The day was set. The invitations were sent far and wide by messenger. And the young king sat on his throne, impatient to see what the people would think up.

Many did not come at all, because they did not know how to come with *and* without a present. Some thought up very clever ways of getting around the puzzle, and some thought up very silly ways.

But what delighted the king most was the young girl who came carrying something very gently and carefully in her two hands.

"Put out your hand," she said to the young king. And he put out his hand.

Then, just as the girl reached out to give the king his present, she opened her hands and a little wild bird flew away.

As Many As—

ONCE there was a king who kept asking riddles of everybody. He wanted to find out who was the cleverest person in the whole country.

Finally, one young fellow gave him so many clever answers that he decided to think up some riddle that would be impossible to answer, and see what the boy would do about that!

When the king said, "What is your father doing?" the boy replied:

"He is making much from little." And the king knew that the man was sowing grain.

When the king said, "What is the swiftest thing in the world?" the boy said:

"Thought."

"What is greenest?"

"The month of May."

"What is deepest?"

"The heart of man."

And thus it went, until one day the king said, "How many hairs are there in my beard?"

This was the riddle he thought no one could possibly answer.

The young fellow said he would go home and come back with the answer tomorrow. The king said, "All right."

Morning came, and when the king looked out the

window, there came the boy riding his donkey up to the palace door.

"Well, how many hairs are there in my beard?" said the king.

"As many as there are in the tail of my donkey," said the boy.

"Wha-at?" cried the king.

"If you don't believe it, we can pull them out and count them: one from your beard, one from his tail, one from your beard, one from his tail—till they are counted."

Over the old woman's hut hangs a crust of bread. The dog barks but cannot reach it. What is it?

THE CRESCENT MOON

Transportation Problem

ONCE there was a man who was set the task of taking a wolf, a goat, and a cabbage across a river. When he came to the river, he found that the boat was so small it would hold one man and only *one other* thing.

What was he to do? How could he take the wolf, the goat, and the cabbage over, one at a time, so that the wolf wouldn't eat the goat and the goat wouldn't eat the cabbage?

Answer:
1. Take the goat over.
2. Take the wolf over and take the goat back.
3. Take the cabbage over (leaving goat behind).
4. Go back and get the goat.
or

1. Take the goat over.
2. Take the cabbage over and take the goat back.
3. Take the wolf over (leaving goat behind).
4. Go back and get the goat.

Wordplay Riddles

Poke out its eyes and it has nothing left but a nose. What is it?

NOISE

What is the biggest room in the world?

ROOM FOR IMPROVEMENT

Who was the greatest actor in the Bible?

SAMSON, BECAUSE HE BROUGHT DOWN THE HOUSE

What did Samson die of?

FALLEN ARCHES

What should you keep after you have given it to someone?

YOUR WORD

What did the carpet say to the floor?

I'VE GOT YOU COVERED!

What did one wall say to the other?

WE'LL MEET AT THE CORNER

What did the earth say when it rained?

IF THIS KEEPS UP, MY NAME IS MUD

Why is a pencil like a riddle?

NO GOOD WITHOUT A POINT

TRICKS

How many helpers did you have yesterday?

TEN

You don't have to say a word to answer this riddle. Just hold up your ten fingers.

Tall Hog

THERE WAS a farmer who took a truckload of fine hogs to the fair. But he kept bragging about the one he hadn't brought. That hog, he said, was so tall that a man couldn't touch its back if he held his hand as high as he could reach.

"Some tall hog," he kept saying. Finally a stranger stepped up and said he would buy that hog.

So the price was agreed on and the stranger paid his money. Then he went home with the farmer to see the hog.

The farmer took the man into the pig house.

"There he is," he said.

"*That* hog?" said the man.

"Sure," said the farmer. "You just reach up as high as you can, and you can't possibly touch its back."

Holding Down the Hat

ONCE a young fellow was walking along a road. He had far to go and no way to get there but to walk. Soon, however, he saw in the distance a man on horseback coming his way. Quickly, he snatched off his hat and held it down tight on the road by the brim.

When the man on horseback came along, he stopped and said, "What are you guarding there under the hat?"

"It is a beautiful golden bird."

"Let me see."

"I don't want it to get away," said the young fellow. "Lend me the horse and I will go fetch a cage—that is, if you will hold down the hat till I get back."

So the stranger got off his horse and carefully held down the hat while the other mounted and rode away.

The road was hot in the sun, but the man sat there, holding down the hat. Time went by—and time went by. And the man sat there, holding down the hat.

At last, at last—he looked. And under the hat was—*nothing*.

When North American Indians tell this story, the dupe is usually tricked into holding up a cliff (which the trickster says will fall), or holding up a rock, or

66

holding up the roof of a cave. And he is finally left holding it up alone while the trickster rides off on the horse "to get help" and, of course, never comes back.

The trick is so dear to the human mind that a variation of it turns up today as a modern parlor trick among boys and girls of high-school and college age.

For any parlor or party trick, of course, there is always a group in the know and one person (at least) who has never heard of the trick before.

To play this trick, those in the know begin very seriously to discuss whether or not it is possible to make a glass of water stick to the ceiling. So one of them gets a tumbler full of water and stands on a chair and holds the glass tight up against the ceiling.

Soon he says that he is tired and asks the unwary one to go get a broom and help him to steady the glass of water against the ceiling with the broom handle.

As soon as the dupe has pushed the broom handle tight up against the bottom of the glass, the fellow on the chair gets down, and everybody goes out of the room and just leaves the dupe there.

What happens?

Try it and see.

Five Dozen Eggs

ONCE a man went to a country market. He found a farmer who had good fresh eggs to sell, and the man said he would buy five dozen.

The farmer had all his eggs in a great big basket. He started to count them out for the man, one by one; but the man said, "Here! I'll count. You fold your arms and hold them while I count them out of the basket."

So the farmer stood up and folded his arms, and the man took the eggs out of the basket, one, two, three, four . . . and piled them up in the farmer's arms until he said, ". . . fifty-nine, sixty."

"There! That's five dozen!" said the man and walked away without another word.

The Horse with His Head Where His Tail Ought To Be

ONCE there was a man who had a horse with his head where his tail ought to be. Anyway, that is what the man told people. And he decided to put him on show and make him earn his keep.

So the man made a sign and nailed it up on his barn.

```
COME IN AND SEE
THE HORSE WITH HIS HEAD
WHERE HIS TAIL OUGHT TO BE
10¢
```

The next day a long line of people queued up outside the barn door. Everybody wanted to see the horse with his head where his tail ought to be.

The man explained that they would have to come in one at a time. He could not have a crowd inside. So the first man paid his dime and went in. In a few minutes he came out grinning and walked away without saying a word to anyone.

So the next man paid his dime and went in. In a few minutes he too came out, grinned at everybody, and walked off.

So the third man paid his dime and went in. Everybody watched to see if he would be grinning too.

70

He was. And he walked away without saying a word.

The people waiting in line got more and more curious. They could hardly wait to get inside and see this wonder.

Finally the last man in line paid his dime and went in. This is what he saw:

There was the horse with his tail to the feed box and his head sticking out the rear of the stall. The man had simply turned him around!

Of course, no one was willing to be the only dupe in town! That is why every man came out grinning and never gave the joke away.

It's a Pleasure!

Adam and Eve and Pinchme
Went down to the river to bathe.
Adam and Eve were drowned.
Who was saved?

WHOEVER quick says "Pinchme" without thinking, gets pinched of course! But almost every schoolchild knows this old trick today. So to disguise it, children sometimes say:

Adam and Eve and Kickmequick
Went down to the river to bathe. . . .

Or Nipmehard or Nipmewell or even Punchme or Treadonmytoes.

Whoever gets taken in by this trick—and gets pinched, punched, nipped, or stepped on—instead of crying or complaining or even getting mad, is supposed to say, "Oh, my! It's a pleasure!" If he does that, he's a real good guy instead of a crybaby.

The Silver Jug

ONCE there was a woman who said it was not fair for all women to be blamed for Eve's curiosity. Many women were not like that. She herself was not curious, for instance. She would never get caught in idle curiosity.

This kind of bragging finally reached the king's ears, and he invited the woman to his palace. She could roam all over the whole place, he said. She could go into any room, look in any closet, any chest, any drawer. There wasn't anywhere she couldn't go or sit or look.

"Except—" said the king, "except in this silver jug."

He placed a beautiful little silver jug on a small table. It had a lid with a little knob on top.

"Don't open the jug," said the king. "That's all I ask. Don't open this one little jug."

"All right," said the woman.

She wandered all over the palace, looking at all the fine things and enjoying herself immensely. Each new room was grander than the one before. But at last she had seen it all, and then there was nothing to do.

It was a pretty silver jug, she thought. She wondered what was in it. Perhaps it contained the rarest thing of all, because it was the only thing the king had warned her not to open.

73

What harm could it do just to look, she thought.
She wouldn't take out what was in there. Just one
peek, and no one would ever know.

So she looked.

And a mouse hopped out.

And the woman SCREAMED and SQUEALED and
jumped on a chair.

And everybody came running to see what was the
matter. So everybody knew—and the king knew.
And nobody said a word! So the woman went home.

SURPRISES AND
ANSWERS

"What makes you so gray, Grampa?" said the little boy.

"MY HAIR"

Did you ever hear the story of the empty box?

NOTHING IN IT

How To Cook a Coot

COOT is the nickname for the scoter duck, a sea duck that lives entirely on fish. Coots are very seldom eaten because their flesh is rank and oily and tough. Most people do not like either the odor or the taste. But it is said that if they are cooked *just right,* they can be very good.

The way to do it is this:

First, pluck and clean the bird just as you would any other fowl.

Boil it for four hours to get rid of the rank, oily taste. Pour off this water, add fresh, and boil for four more hours to get rid of the rest of the flavor.

Next, put a brick inside the bird and bake in the oven until done.

How long? When the brick is soft, it is done.

Then throw away the coot and eat the brick.

Growing Pains

ONCE there was a little boy who suddenly started to grow tall. He grew so fast even his shadow could not keep up with him.

He grew and he grew and kept on growing, and then one day he had to get up on a chair to button his collar.

Finally—the day the top of his head grew out through the top of his hat—his mother said, "Heavens, Sammy! You'll have to start eating lard."

"What for?" said the boy.

"Shortening."

Hungry Hog

ONCE there was a hog so hungry that he ate two sticks of dynamite.

He ate the first one all right and was still hungry, so he started in on the second. And while he was crunching away on the second, he blew up.

It was a fearful explosion. People heard it clear into town. It caved in one side of the barn, broke all the windows in the farmer's house, killed two mules, one cow, and three chickens.

And that was a mighty sick hog.

Through the Needle's Eye

IN THE SMALL Eskimo village of Unisak on the edge of Bering Strait, once lived a little boy with his grandmother. Every day the boy walked along the shore to gather seaweed and he took all that he found home for them to eat.

One day he was walking along the shore singing a little song:

> I am walking along the shore
> I am getting seaweed
> The waves splash my knees
> I am getting seaweed
> I put it in my shirt
> I carry it home
> I am getting seaweed
> And I carry it home

It was just his own little song that he sang to himself alone on the edge of the water. And that day he found so much seaweed that he had a heavy load.

He kept gathering more and more seaweed and stuffing it inside his shirt. The shirt bulged out all around the little boy, and still he kept jamming more into it. Finally he looked like a round ball on two little feet. He was as wide as he was tall.

When he got home he stood in front of the little

house and wondered how he would ever get through
the little, low narrow door.

"Ho!" he called out.

"Ho!" cried the grandmother inside.

"I have seaweed," said the boy.

"Good!"

"I have too much!"

"Good!"

"How can I get in the house?"

"Come in as if through the eye of a needle."

"What needle?"

"This one."

The old grandmother stuck a needle out through
the door and the boy walked through it with his load.

That's all.

I'll Tell Her

EVERYBODY was in swimming that bright day: grown-ups and children—boys and girls. Some of the people were expert swimmers; some were learners; and some were the kind who just stood knee-deep and shivered. A little stone wharf jutted out into the water alongside the place.

The experts were diving from the end of the wharf. They loved diving down into a deep spot among the black rocks, not a place for a beginner.

One little boy, nine years old, who was already a good swimmer, decided that *today* he was going to dive. His mother was not there, and the hostess (whose little beach and wharf it was) said, "Oh, don't dive, Kennie! I don't want to have to tell your mother you dove off my wharf and got drowned!"

"Never mind. I'll tell her!" said Kennie, and in he went.

Deaf Men and Their Answers

1. Fence Post

ONCE there was a deaf man working on a fence post, cutting and shaping it to the right size for his purpose.

He saw a man coming along the road and thought to himself: Now, he'll ask me what I'm making, and I'll say "fence post." Then he'll say, "How long are you going to make it?" And I'll say, "Four feet." Then he'll say, "Well, good day to you," and walk off, and I'll say, "The same to you, sir!" and he'll never know that he was talking to a deaf man.

So he worked busily on his fence post, and soon the stranger stopped beside him.

"A beautiful morning we're having," he said.

"Fence post," said the deaf man.

"Can you tell me how far it is to the next town?"

"Four feet."

The stranger stared.

"You're a fool!" he said.

"The same to you, sir," said the deaf man and went happily on with his work.

2. *Bedside Visit*

One day the deaf man went to call on a sick friend. He imagined what his friend might say and made up the proper answers. When he got to the house he inquired for his sick friend. Well, he was very sick, the deaf man was told, but he could go in to see him.

So he went into the room and stood by the side of the bed.

"How are you?" he said.

"Oh, I am going to die."

"Thank God for that! What have you eaten?"

"Poison, I guess."

"Just what you need!—Well, good day."

3. *Thirsty*

Next is the story of two men who were a little bit deaf. Each one could hear, but each was just deaf enough that he could never hear anything quite right.

One day they were taking an auto trip together. As they passed through a pretty little town, one said, "What town is this?"

"I think this is Wesley."

"Oh, I thought it was Thursday."

"So am I. Let's stop and have a drink!"

"This is the end,"
said the
little dog
as he chased
his tail.

Author's Notes and Bibliography

The abbreviations used in this section and in the Bibliography are:

FCBCNCF   *Frank C. Brown Collection of North Carolina Folklore*
FFC   *Folklore Fellows Communications*
JAF   *Journal of American Folklore*
MAFS   *Memoirs of the American Folklore Society*
SFQ   *Southern Folklore Quarterly*
TAPS   *Transactions of the American Philosophical Society*
WF   *Western Folklore*

The numbers in parentheses are the motif numbers as given in Stith Thompson's *Motif-Index of Folk Literature.*

NOODLES

The Man with the Chair on His Head. This story is a composite of the tale as recorded in the *FCBCNCF* 1:698 and by A. M. Bacon from Virginia. It has been given the motif number J1762.4. The earliest version was collected by A. M. Bacon among Virginia Negroes sometime between 1894–1899. (See A. M. Bacon and E. C. Parsons: Folk-Lore from Elizabeth City County, Virginia, *JAF* 35:301, #73.) The North Carolina variant is dated 1928–1929.

Dreams. The dream of being chased by a bear and henceforth taking the dog to bed is mentioned in Clouston: *The Book of Noodles,* p. 4, as an ancient Greek jest. In the Greek anecdote, however, the hunter was chased by a wild boar. The man who took the mirror to bed to find out if he slept with his mouth open (J1936.1) is also a Greek jest mentioned by Clouston, p. 9. E. W. Baughman reports it as current in England.

    The story of the hunters and their dreams is a French-Canadian tale collected by Marius Barbeau in the province of Quebec in 1914 from narrators who said it was a very ancient story. It is published in Barbeau: Contes Populaires Canadiens, *JAF* 29:134–135, and is freely translated here. This too is a Turkish fourteenth-century Khoja Nasreddin anecdote which spread, probably via Italy and Spain, throughout Europe and came to America with the first colonists and later settlers.

    There are Italian, Spanish, French, German, and English versions, as well as Icelandic and Russian. Versions from India and Japan have been collected and also Jewish variants. Archer Taylor reported a versified form from St. Louis in 1921, in which the best dreamer wins the baloney. Vance Randolph reports the tale from Arkansas about three boys in the woods hunting possum. They caught such a *little* possum that they agreed the dreamer of the best dream could have it all. See Randolph's Folktales from Arkansas, *JAF* 65:161. A Utah version is reported by L. A. Hubbard in *WF* 15:128–130. A. H. Fauset found it in the form of an

Englishman-Scotchman-Irishman story among Nova Scotia Negroes. See his Folklore from Nova Scotia, *MAFS* 24:54.

The most familiar form of the story tells of three travelers who agreed that whichever one of them dreamed the most wonderful dream should have their last loaf of bread. The third man ate the bread in the night and said he dreamed the other two were dead and didn't need it. This is the form that gives the motif its label: dream bread (K444).

Do It Yourself. This anecdote is based on the well-known folktale motif X1731.2.1 (man falls and is buried in earth; goes for spade and digs himself out), told with varying details all over Europe and America. It is reported from Germany and Flanders of a man who fell out of a balloon. E. E. Gardner reports it from Schoharie County, New York, as an incident in the life of a Tim Murphy who jumped off a cliff to escape a band of approaching Indians. See her Folk-Lore from Schoharie County, New York, *JAF* 27:305. She cites it also as a Serbian tale occurring in Lang's *Violet Fairy Book*, p. 21. This is also one of the favorite jokes people tell about an Irishman.

Catching the Thief. This is an ancient Greek jest, cited by Clouston in *The Book of Noodles*, p. 14. Waiting for the thief to return for the pillow (bolster) is motif J2214.3.2.

Telling the Horses Apart. This anecdote is based on motif J2722 in the *Motif-Index*, citing E. W. Baughman: A Comparative Study of the Folktales of England and North America, Indiana University dissertation, 1954.

Shoes Don't Match. This story is retold from one told to Edward Sapir by Hsü T'sau Hwa in 1923 as a bit of Chinese folk humor: the kind of thing, he said, that passes by word of mouth from generation to generation without ever getting written down. See Edward Sapir and Hsü T'sau Hwa: Humor of the Chinese Folk, *JAF* 36:31–35 (1923).

Trip to Town. Going to town in the wheelbarrow is a local anecdote from Shelburne County, Nova Scotia, told to me by Mr. Kenneth Coffin of Coffinscroft; and "it happened right here."

As tired as if he had walked is motif J1946, with reference to Albert Wesselski's edition of Heinrich Bebel's *Schwänke*, 2 vols., Munich, 1907.

The Wrong Man. This story is based on an ancient Greek noodle story as told in Clouston's *Book of Noodles*, p. 6. The Greeks loved to tell jokes about learned men (scholars, pedants), and our absent-minded-professor jokes today are direct descendants of these old pedant jests.

Silly John. These few episodes from the many told about Silly John or Jean Sot are based on tellings in Alcée Fortier: Louisiana Folk-Tales, *MAFS* 2:63–69 and Calvin Claudel: Foolish John Tales from the French Folklore of Louisiana, *SFQ* 12:158, 163.

The Wise Men of Gotham. These stories about the wise men of Gotham are based on the presentation given in Clouston: *The Book of Noodles*, pp. 21, 26–27, 28–33. The twenty anecdotes recounting the foolishnesses of the men of Gotham were first collected and printed in England in 1630, but they were known in oral tradition before that, for *the foles of Gotham* are familiarly referred to in the *Widmark Miracle Plays,* a manuscript of the mid-fifteenth century. The King John episode, of course, is supposed to have occurred in the thirteenth century.

The story of the pent cuckoo (J1904.2, J1904.2.1) comprises probably one of the best-known of all noodle motifs; it is certainly one of the most famous of the Gothamite enterprises. The story of the twelve men who could not count themselves (J2030) is known in India and Ceylon, Indonesia, Russia, Scandinavia, Switzerland, France, Germany, and other parts of northern Europe. It is told in China and by the Bicol people of southeastern Luzon in the Philippine Islands. And it is also one of the Turkish Khoja Nasreddin jests.

Drowning the Eel. This story is retold from the version in Clouston's *Book of Noodles,* pp. 33–34. It falls into the general category of stories about animals (or objects) being absurdly punished (J1860). Specifically it involves motif J1900: absurd disregard of animal's nature or habits plus motif K581: animal punished by being placed in its natural environment. The Negro story (both African and New World Negro) familiar to most readers through Joel Chandler Harris's *Uncle Remus,* in which Turtle's frantic plea not to be thrown in the water results in his captors doing just that (K581.1), is perhaps the most famous of these.

A Fine Cheese. This story is retold from Clouston's *Book of Noodles,* pp. 44–45. He adds that it is told of the people of Wiltshire, England, too, who were dubbed *moon-rakers* because of the incident. The Lithuanian moon riddle is reported by Archer Taylor: Collection of Mongolian Riddles, *TAPS* 44, pt.3:400.

Lightening the Load. This anecdote is retold from Clouston: *The Book of Noodles,* pp. 19–20. Relieving the beast of burden is motif J1874. Rider puts sack on his own shoulder to relieve the ass (J1874.1) is one of the fourteenth-century Turkish Khoja Nasreddin jests; and it is included in Poggio Bracciolini's *Facezie* (fifteenth century). It has since swept through Europe: Italy, Germany, England. In England this kindhearted act is credited to a man of Norfolk as well as to a Gothamite.

The story of the Irishman in the boat was being told in England in the nineteenth century and has since established itself in the United States wherever the Irishman jokes have been popular. Clouston cites a Ceylon variant of the lightening the load in the boat incident (p. 68*n*1).

I Was Wondering. This small story comprises the European motif J2377 (the philosophical watchman) and is classified in the general category of anecdotes about inquisitive fools. There is a sly moral behind it.

Rescuing the Moon. This small story, which has been told many times in many rural places as being the escapade of some local nitwit, is one of the old Turkish Khoja Nasreddin jokes about fools and their foolish undertakings. Rescuing the moon is motif J1791.2. It is known and told in Denmark. It was familiar among Southern United States Negroes in the nineteenth century and turns up in Harris's *Nights with Uncle Remus.*

RIDDLES

The *bald-head riddle* is probably one of the most popular riddles in the world. Sometimes the answer to it is "One eye" or "One leg." It is found in *The Booke of Merry Riddles,* published in 1629, but it is undoubtedly much older than that. It is reported, in diverse wordings, from all parts of England, Scotland, Wales, and Ireland, from Holland and Flanders, Denmark, Norway, and Sweden, and also Spain. It is a familiar riddle in Newfoundland and Nova Scotia. In the United States it has been collected in Virginia, North Carolina, South Carolina, Tennessee, Indiana, New Hampshire, the Ozarks, and in New Orleans, New York, and Pennsylvania. It is widespread among Southern Negroes, including those of the Carolina Sea Islands, and is known to Jamaica Negroes also. See Archer Taylor: *English Riddles from Oral Tradition,* pp. 649, 858–859.

The Riddle of the Sphinx is one of the oldest and probably the most famous riddle in the world. It is certainly the most basic of all riddles, for the answer is man himself. It contains motifs H541.1 (Sphinx propounds riddle on pain of death) and C822 (solving Sphinx's riddle: Sphinx perishes). The riddle itself is H761.

The place and moment of the riddle's origin no one knows. It is so widespread, however, that some scholars feel that it may have cropped up independently in such farflung cultures as those of Indonesia, Polynesia, Melanesia (Fiji), for instance, where parallels are found.

Archer Taylor thinks that a reference to the Sphinx's riddle by the Greek poet Asclepiades in the third century B.C. is the first mention of it in writing, unless Hesiod knew it (eighth century B.C.) and was referring to it when he described a man with a stick in a snowstorm as three-legged. See Taylor: *English Riddles from Oral Tradition,* pp. 20–24.

The riddle itself, minus the trappings of the Sphinx story, is widespread. It turns up, in slightly varied wordings, widely in Europe, fairly often in England, and among the Scottish Gaels. A Hungarian version has almost the identical wording of the riddle in the Greek story. It has been collected in its simplest form among Negroes of Virginia and Tennessee and seems to be widely familiar among Negroes of the Southern United States. It is also known in parts of Canada, the Antilles, and in South America.

The Opies picked up a riddle among English schoolchildren that goes: *Walks on four feet/ On two feet, on three/ The more feet it walks on/ The weaker it be/* to which the answer is Man. See their *Lore and Language of Schoolchildren,* p. 76.

Seven Sons. This story is a rare one involving a neck riddle. Neck riddles *save necks;* that is, they save lives. There are tales of a man about to be hanged for theft or some other crime, who will escape the death penalty if he can make up a riddle that the king (judge, executioner) cannot answer (H542). There is a Spanish folktale about a man who frees his father by concocting a riddle that the king cannot answer (R154.2.1).

This small story of the seven sons is based on an Ozark mountain riddle collected by Vance Randolph. See Randolph and Stradley: Ozark Mountain Riddles, *JAF* 47:87.

E. C. Parsons reported the same neck-riddle tale from the Negroes of Long Island in the Bahamas in 1928. In this case the old woman said, "The living jumped out of the dead to save the life of the seventh son." What she had seen was a little dog jump out of the carcass of a dead cow. See Parsons: Spirituals and Other Folklore from the Bahamas, *JAF* 41:479.

The Full Moon. This is a riddle story about the king and the clever, clever girl. It bears motif number H582.1.1 and falls into the general group of stories based on enigmatic statements. It is known in Germany and Arabia, and an African analogue is reported.

Outriddling the Princess. This story is based on no one folktale in any specific collection. It is built up by the author around the Eurasian motif H551: princess offered in marriage to youth who can outriddle her. As told here it follows the type and uses the folk riddles typical of the tale wherever found. The theme itself goes back to the ancient Greeks; and the story, with varying detail, is popular across northern Europe from Russia to the British Isles. There is a version from the Punjab, India; and Verrier Elwin reports two tales from the Baiga people of Middle India containing the related motif H511: princess offered to correct guesser. See his *Myths of Middle India,* p. 142.

The riddles vary, of course, with the tellings, but the ones used here are typical. The question about the distance from one end of the earth to the other is motif H681.1.1. The six legs, four ears, two faces riddle is motif H744; and the seven tongues in one head riddle is H793. The riddle likening the sun to a bird in the cypress trees is an ancient Persian metaphorical riddle. The question how far to the bottom of the ocean with its stone's throw answer bears motif number H681.4.1; the distance from heaven to earth being one step is H682.1.9.

The final bit of repartee between the boy and the princess about her red lips and cooking the egg is motif H507.1.0.1: princess defeated in repartee by means of object accidentally picked up.

The Blind Men and the Elephant. This is a very old Oriental puzzle riddle, known especially, of course, wherever elephants are domesticated and are part of the daily life of the people; but it is also widespread in European countries. See Archer Taylor: *English Riddles from Oral Tradition,* p. 582*n*11 and Thompson-Balys: *Oral Tales of India,* under J1761.10.

The House Without Eyes or Ears. There is a small group of folktales from India, and quite widespread in Europe, dealing with the clever youth or maiden who answers the king's questions in riddles (H583). The story about the house with neither eyes nor ears comprises motif H583.8.

With and Without. The king's invitation to the populace to come to the feast *with and without a present* falls in the general category of tales dealing with tests of resourcefulness. The little bird set free at the moment of bestowal is motif H1056.

As Many As—is another story built up by the author, using a handful of folk riddles in the test-of-cleverness framework. The riddle about sowing grain is motif H583.2.2; the swiftest thing in the world (thought) is motif H632.1; the greenest (May) is H646.1; the deepest (the heart of man) is H643.1. The question, "How many hairs are there in my beard?" and its answer comprise motif H703.1.

Transportation Problem. This little problem is one of the old and famous tests of resourcefulness (motif H506.3) of European folklore.

The *crescent-moon riddle* is one of the old peasant riddles mentioned in Y. M. Sokolov: *Russian Folklore,* p. 287.

TRICKS

Tall Hog. This trick is listed as motif K196.2 (tall hog) in the *Motif-Index,* citing E. W. Baughman: A Comparative Study of the Folktales of England and North America, Indiana University dissertation, 1954.

Holding Down the Hat (K1252) is a popular and widespread Asiatic-European folktale told from Russia to the Cape Verde Islands. For a Portuguese version, see the final episode in Delfina Peixoto: The King's Counselors: A Portuguese Folktale, *California Folklore Quarterly* 2:31–34 (1943). The tale is found also in Java, other parts of Indonesia, and Indochina. North American Indian versions, as mentioned, present the trickster leaving the dupe holding *up* the cliff, the rock, the roof, etc., while he rides off on the horse and is never seen again. In this form, too, the motif is found among certain South African Negro peoples. See Parsons: Folklore from the Cape Verde Islands, *MAFS* 15:1:54; Sokolov: *Russian Folklore,* p. 475. For discussion, see Thompson: *The Folktale,* p. 202. For the description of the party trick with the glass of water and the broom handle, I am indebted to Mr. Benjamin Doane of Halifax, Nova Scotia.

Five Dozen Eggs. This tale is retold from Loomis: Some Folklore of Yankee Genius, 1831–1863, *WF* 6:341, citing the *Boston Transcript,* Aug. 13, 1831.

The Horse with His Head Where His Tail Ought To Be. This story is one more proof that people all over the world love the same jokes and play the same pranks almost everywhere—and *have* for centuries. It is told in the little towns and villages of Europe as a trick pulled by so and so, usually the local wag. And it is told all over the United States in rural districts as a local happening. The man is usually named, and the teller's father knew him.

Clouston, in his *Popular Tales and Fictions* (vol. 1, p. 52), citing Ralston, traces the story to Persia and to the Tyl Eulenspiegel stories of the early sixteenth century. It is probably even earlier, since so popular a tricksy hero as Tyl would have many, many stories told about him that were earlier told about less famous persons.

It's a Pleasure. The origin of this riddle trick has not been determined. It was part of my childhood lore, and I think every child I ever knew in the lower grades also knew it. It was part of my mother's and part of my father's childhood lore; and they grew up as far apart as South Carolina and Nova Scotia. The Opies give eleven variants of it in their *Lore and Language of Schoolchildren,* pp. 59–60, and report it from all over the British Isles, from Holland, France, and Spain, and from East Texas. For its age, they give a tentative date of 1855. It must surely be older than this, because my Nova Scotia grandfather, born in 1823, also knew it.

The Silver Jug. This story is based on motif H1554.1 (test of curiosity: mouse in jug), one of many falling in the category of tests devised to discover a person's true character. It is fairly common in European folktales and is reported from Germany, Denmark, and Spain. There is a Jewish version, and it turns up also in medieval exempla.

SURPRISES AND ANSWERS

How To Cook a Coot. This has been a common joke for generations in the oral tradition of the fishermen of the south shore of Nova Scotia. It was told to me by Mr. Donald Robertson of Shelburne, Nova Scotia, during an evening of story-swapping. It is perhaps a distant cousin to the American tough-goose motif (X1258.2).

Growing Pains. This anecdote is put together from four Jonathanisms from the collection compiled by C. Grant Loomis. See his Jonathanisms: American Epigrammatic Hyperbole, *WF* 6: 212–213, citing *Yankee Blade*, December 31, 1842; April 1, 1843; May 20, 1848; and *Porter's Spirit of the Times* 6, #15, New York, 1859.

Hungry Hog. This item is based on one in Folklore in the News, *WF* 6:281.

Through the Needle's Eye. This story is based on a tale collected by Waldemar Bogoras and published in The Eskimo of Siberia, *Publications of the Jesup North Pacific Expedition,* vol. 8, pt. 3, Leiden and New York, 1913, p. 420.

I'll Tell Her. This is an eye-witness and ear-witness story told for the first time in this book. But what do you bet that inside a year some doting grandma will be telling it about her smart little darling, or some uncle will be bragging about the quick answer made by his brother's clever kid! This is the way of the folk with a joke.

Deaf Men and Their Answers. The first of these stories, "Fence Post," was told to me by my cousins when I was a child. It is a much older joke than that, however. Workman answers traveler with remarks about his work is motif X111.10. It is known to have been widespread and popular in Europe for many generations. The kind of work and the specific answers, of course, vary from group to group and locale to locale. But it is the same old joke everywhere.

The story of the deaf man's visit to a sick friend is based on motif X111.9. This anecdote also is told widely in Europe, and versions of it have been recorded in India. The joke about the two friends mistaking the words *Wesley* and *Thursday* for *Wednesday* and *thirsty* is purely American. It is given as motif X111.15 in the *Motif-Index,* citing E. W. Baughman: A Comparative Study of the Folktales of England and North America, Indiana University dissertation, 1954.

BIBLIOGRAPHY

Antti Aarne and Stith Thompson: Types of the Folk-Tale, *FFC* 74 (1928)
A. M. Bacon and E. C. Parsons: Folk-Lore from Elizabeth City County, Virginia, *JAF* 35:250–327 (1922)
Marius Barbeau: Contes Populaires Canadiens, *JAF* 29:1–151 (1916)
Calvin Claudel: Foolish John Tales from the French Folklore of Louisiana, *SFQ* 12:151–165 (1948)
W. A. Clouston: *The Book of Noodles,* Elliot Stock, London, 1888
————: *Popular Tales and Fictions,* 2 vols., William Blackwood and Sons, Edinburgh and London, 1887
Verrier Elwin: *Myths of Middle India,* Oxford University Press, 1949
A. H. Fauset: Negro Folklore from the South, *JAF* 40:213–303 (1927)
————: Folklore from Nova Scotia, *MAFS* 24 (1931)
Folklore in the News, *WF* 6:281 (1947)
Alcée Fortier: Louisiana Folk-Tales, *MAFS* 2:63–69 (1895)
FCBCNCF, vol. 1, Duke University Press, Durham, 1952
E. E. Gardner: Folk-Lore from Schoharie County, New York, *JAF* 27:304–325 (1914)
L. A. Hubbard: A Utah Version of the Three Dreams, *WF* 15:128–130 (1956)
Maria Leach: *The Rainbow Book of American Folk Tales and Legends,* The World Publishing Company, Cleveland and New York, 1958
C. Grant Loomis: Some Folklore of Yankee Genius, 1831–1863, *WF* 6:341–350 (1947)
————: Jonathanisms: American Epigrammatic Hyperbole, *ibid:* 211–227
Iona and Peter Opie: *The Lore and Language of Schoolchildren,* Oxford University Press, Oxford, 1959
Elsie Clews Parsons: Folklore from Aiken, South Carolina, *JAF* 34:36 (1921)
————: Spirituals and Other Folklore from the Bahamas, *JAF* 41:453–524 (1928)
Vance Randolph: Folktales from Arkansas, *JAF* 65:161 (1952)
———— and Isabel Stradley: Ozark Mountain Riddles, *JAF* 47:81–89 (1934)
Y. M. Sokolov: *Russian Folklore,* Macmillan Company, New York, 1950
Archer Taylor: The Dream Bread Story Once More, *JAF* 34:327–328 (1921)
————: *English Riddles from Oral Tradition,* University of California Press, Berkeley and Los Angeles, 1951
————: Collection of Mongolian Riddles, *TAPS* 44, pt.3:400 (1954)
Stith Thompson: *The Folktale,* Dryden Press, New York, 1946
————: *Motif-Index of Folk Literature,* 6 vols., Indiana University Press, Bloomington, 1955–1958
———— and Jonas Balys: *Oral Tales of India,* Indiana University Press, Bloomington, 1958

96